The Soul Letters Yo

- A 3-part

C000101598

Vol 2: You Are The Medicine

The return to Connection...

You are never
alone.
Call upon you
guides +
ancestors
with love,
Natacha
B
July 22

Copyright 2021 © Natacha Dauphin
All Rights Reserved

The right of Natacha Dauphin to be the author of this work has been asserted in accordance with the Copyright, Designs and Patents Act 1988.

This is the first edition publishing through KDP (February 2021) and all rights remain with the author Natacha Dauphin.

No part of this publication may be reproduced, stored or transmitted in any form or by any means without prior written consent from the author.

Enquiries: honouringyourcreativefire@gmail.com

ISBN: 9798577381370

Contents

Prologue

We live in a time and society that forever mirror back a distorted picture.

Day after day, we are made to think that we have no power, no choice, no magic, no medicine.

This is a huge lie.

No matter where we are on our journey, we have the right, ability and resources to strive, thrive, blossom and heal.

Our healing balm is faithfully waiting for us and it will do so until our last breath.

If you seek peace, balance, alignment, vitality, energy, joy, comfort, space, encouragement, company, help, it is not that you are broken, or even that there is something wrong with you; rather the opposite. It is that you are remembering your knowing, your wisdom. It is that you are finally reconnecting with all the parts of yourself - the shiny, the dark, the glittery, the opaque.

By accepting them all for what they are, you can let go of the ones that no longer serve you and keep you small. More importantly you do this from a place of awareness and free will rather than guilt or shame.

You embrace the cycles of life, the processes, the processing.

You finally welcome the miracle that you are and invite all the pieces of yourself to participate in this extraordinary adventure called life.

May this second volume of *The Soul Letters You Never Received* series remind you of your birthright to be who you are, to reclaim your sovereignty, to choose the person you want to be and the life you desire to live.

Sometimes,
All we need

Is to feel
The gentle breeze
On our face,

Imagine
The softness
Of a rainbow,

Smell
The sweetness
Of a flower,

To remember

Who we are,
Where we come from,
And where we are going.

The Gift Of Presence, An Ecstatic Vibration

Today,

Is the focus and goal.

Tomorrow,

The ever-changing landscape of vision.

Giggles

Are

So

Joyful

And

Giggly.

Will

You

Dare

To

Giggle

With

Me?

When you feel

Irritated

By small things,

You are most likely

Not attending

To what really matters

To your soul

And what makes

Your heart sing.

It moves me to tears
To think back
To how much
You believed in me.

And although you are gone,
Neither the belief
Nor the feelings
Change.

They will
Never change.

They are imprinted and alive
In all the sacred parts of my being.

In this very moment,
You still believe in me,
With an extra twinkle
In your starry eyes
And the Milky Way
Inside your heart.

Just be here,
Really here.

There is so much sweetness

In this sacred space,
In this sacred time.

Thank you
For the flowers.

Thank you
For the nectar.

Thank you
For the dance.

You are not just present
In my memories.

You are present
Here and now.

Your spirit is strong.

I am in awe
Of this life.

I bow to her
In profound
Gratitude.

The now

Gets rid of

Any distortion.

I am grateful

For my connection

To the earth,

Her wisdom,

Her knowledge,

And the love

She breathes into my being,

Each day.

Everything
About this moment
Is perfect.

It is divine
And it is earthly.

It is absolutely yummy.

The pearl of presence
And the pearl of gratitude

Are the most precious pearls

You will ever discover,
You will ever be offered.

I love

Watching

The snow fall.

Huge

Teachings

Come

From

Planting

An

Acorn.

Plug yourself back
Into the ground
When you need
To recharge.

Some things
Are
That simple.

Show up,

Commit,

Put the work in,

Honour the process.

The rest

Will take care of itself.

Today is a new day.

Everything about it awaits,
With excitement,

To be discovered
And lived.

In my dreams
I finally meet
The buried parts of myself.

There,
I am guided
To work with them,
Shift and heal.

How incredible is this?

I am so deeply grateful.

I sink

Further

Into

The raw

And soft

Feeling

Of surrender

And playfulness.

You visit me
In my dreams.

The following morning,
My heart beats
Stronger.

The comfort
Of your presence
In my heart,
In my chest,
Is perhaps the most uncanny feeling
I have ever experienced.

The melting
And expansion
Into oneness
Of your love for me,
And my love for you,
Despite your angel wings
And my human legs,
Moves me to tears.

I honestly
Can no longer distinguish
My love from your love,
Your love from my love.

And this is bliss.

Skip, dance, run.

Feel the ecstasy
Of movement
And breath
Flowing through you.

Feel the joy
Of them
Dancing within
And around you.

Clarity will prevail.

Nothing is a threat.
Nothing is a problem.

Everything
Simply is.

Honour that.

Pay attention to the amazing sound
Emerging from the depths of your belly,
Rising from the grandeur of your soul.

Resonating
Vibrating
Reverberating
Against the walls of your body,
Within the temple of your heart,
And all around you,

Filling the room with tingles of frequencies.

Observe how contagious this is,
How easily and playfully
The ripples of laughter enliven the space
And change everything into magic.

Imagine
How the spirits,
The gods,
The ancestors

Experience

These ripples echoing

Against each and every surface of the universe.

How glorious it must sound,

How delighted they must be.

Release

The tired breath

Of old dreams

And outdated visions

So that new life

And vitality

Can birth

Freshly aligned ones.

A thick layer of frost
Has covered the colours,
The shapes, the noise,
Turning our entire universe
Into a sparkling field of magic.

Be a witness,
Be an active observer.

What can possibly be more sacred
Than to offer
Our unconditional presence
To this moment?

The pink Himalayan salt lamp
Dances on the table.

The energy weaves
Invisible beauty through the air.

Pause
Breathe

Center

Connect

Be grateful.

Magic is entering you.

I can hear

The tiny stream

Running

Through the stones,

Smiling

Through the cracks.

It is celebrating

Me paying attention.

I will hug

My darkness

Until it no longer

Feels abandoned.

All that is needed
Is already in the garden,

The dead branches
Ready to offer themselves
To the ground, to the embers,

The seeds as promises of new life,

The shade protecting
What is vulnerable and delicate,

The sun igniting
All that has been asleep,

The magic infusing
The mysteries about to unfold,

With extra glitter.

An ounce of mischief
Will take you a long way.

It will help you access
Your free spirit
And essence.

Gratitude

Is one of the most powerful

Alchemist

I have ever encountered.

It changes

And transforms

Any negative tendencies, thoughts, energy

Into openness, love and acceptance,

Paving the way

For both

You and life

To fully blossom

And embrace

Each other.

Notice
When the energy
Isn't clear.

And clear it.

You have all it takes to do so.

The wolf and the bear
Call to me,

As if I were one of them,
As if they were one of me,

As if I were them,
As if they were me.

The smell
Of incense,
The cat purr,
The cosiness
Of a warm blanket.

Feel the gentle cocooning
Of this sacred moment
When the sun dances its way
To the other side.

The other side - so far and yet so near.

The threads of light connecting us all...

Beyond linear time,
Distance
And the illusion
Of separation.

Feel the arms
Of the evening

Hugging you,

Rocking you,

To a different vibration,

To a higher frequency.

Sense the glorious comfort of the moon

Stroking your soul

Back to now,

Filling the infinite realm of eternity

With the perfume

Of impermanence.

If I can just
Hold on
A bit longer
To this sense
Of wonder,
I will be OK.

Breathe deeply.

Feel Mother Earth
Under the soles of your feet,
Supporting you,
Guiding you.

Feel her cradling you.

If you fall,
Honour that fall.

Whatever you do,
Do not pretend,
Do not live a lie.

Know that you are never alone
And that all is as it should be.

You will be given that helping hand.

Trust me,

I promise.

It is amazing what you end up knowing
- like really knowing,
When you take the time
To connect
To the earth
Before standing
Back up again.

This too, is pure alchemy.

Magic moments in time,
Glimpses of heaven,
Displayed in full attire.

Aliveness and laughter
To sweep through
Our tired steps and stutter.

Gratitude
Filling the air,
Filling the vessel.

The essence of innocence
Remains,
Survives,
Thrives,
Despite the threatening chains
Of dysfunctional systems,
Dismantled collective integrity,
And distorted reality.

Magic moments in time,

Glimpses of heaven,
Displayed in full attire

Filling the air,
Filling the vessel.

We are of the earth
We are of the stars

We are from here
We are from afar.

What really excites me

Is to dive deep

Into inner and outer

Landscapes,

Only to find

That they are

One and the same.

The gift
Of presence
Landed
On my heart
Today.

I bow to it,
I honour it,

And let it fly away.

I am learning to howl again.

I am learning to sway and rock,
Until I can feel the spirits
Circling around me,

Until I can open the door
To their second home,

The one within me.

I keep waking up

With the uncanny feeling

Of diving

Into my own heart.

There is space
In my heart
For all feelings
To be felt
And honoured,

Space for
The confusion,
The clarity,
The hopes,
The regrets,
The disappointments,
The celebrations.

There is space
In my heart
For all to be

Just as it is.

I decided to end all wars
With and within myself.

It is not that hard really.

I just stopped giving
Both sides weapons.

Fists wear out fast.

You can too.

Sit,
Breathe through it all,
And wait
For the storm
To pass,
For the battle
To die out.

Trust

That by committing,

By putting the work in,

The path

To your manifested dreams

Is being paved.

Through breaking a bit more open,
My heart is able to let go
Of what was wedged deep down
But no longer serves me.

For this too,
I am grateful.

I used to judge myself
For daydreaming.

Now I lift a glass
To this magical journey
From which anything
Can continue
To be created.

Don't be afraid
To sink into
The unknown,
The uncomfortable,
The uncertain.

Right there,
In that transition,
Lies your most precious trampoline,
Your next opportunity
To bounce back.

Anything

Can be

Breathed

Through.

We just forget.

The beat
Of the drum
Contains
All heartbeats,

Just as the beat
Of the heart
Contains
All drumbeats.

It is a misconception
To think
We need to give up
The stars, planets and galaxies
In order to really
Land here
On earth.

You will soon find
That the more
You become one
With the earth,
The more
You have access
To the galactic world
You always belonged to.

Dive into the eclipse itself.

There
You will meet
All that is
Currently
And eternally
Playing and displaying
Itself
In your life.

I didn't realize

To what extent

Each word,

Each act of kindness

Can be a magic potion,

Until you sat with me,

Kissed my tears away,

And said with your soft touch,

"It's OK. You are loved."

Our embrace

Was always

About sinking

Into the now.

Each act of kindness
Changes not just one life
But two, or three,
Or even an infinity of lives.

Remember this
When you feel
Worthless and unworthy.

You cannot fill my emptiness,

But you can help it
Feel spacious
And inviting

Rather than scary
And oppressive

So that I may
Dare
Enter it
And create
My own
Love revolution.

If you come to me
With a broken heart,

I will take you
By the river,
I will sit you
Against a tree trunk,
I will kneel quietly
By your side

And wait with you
For as long as
It takes you
To hear
Spirit's healing
Whispers.

I remember the day
You found it easy
To just be.

This made me
Profoundly
Happy.

Prayers To Self, You, And The Universe

I light
A candle,

Knowing
A part
Of you

Is still
With me.

Thank you
For holding
My hand,

Thank you
For holding
My dreams,

Thank you
For holding
My drum,

Thank you
For holding
My heart.

I love you.

I am overflowing
With tears of gratitude.

We are one.

I have no evidence.

Yet,
I have no doubt.

Dear Spirits,

Know
That my love for you
Is deep
And my faith in you
Is strong.

Trust
That I will never
Forget you.

Believe
That I will never
Abandon you.

Just as I know,
You will never
Forget me,
You will never
Abandon me.

May I embrace change

In the way the river embraces
The flow of her waters
Without having to know
Their final destination,

In the way the snow does not question
The relevance of her existence
Because she will soon melt way,

In the way the wind cleanses
Everything it touches
Without needing to be held or praised.

May I be the solid mountain that I am
While being blessed
With unconditional love
For all other sacred elements.

I have a book
To give birth to,
A song to share,
A drum to beat.

Join me,
Create with me,
Be my partner.

I welcome you
And my beautiful spirit guides.

I cannot do this alone.

I need to co-create
With the ones beyond the veil.

I am co-creating
With the ones beyond the veil.

Aho.

Thank you
For finding your way to me
Through my dreams.

Thank you
For telling me so clearly
That you love me.

Thank you
For believing
In me.

Thank you
For never giving up
On me.

When I am silent
Enough,
I can hear
Your hidden
Whispers.

Shake off the old,
Shake off the residues.

Hit the drum.

Get drunk
On its rhythms,
Its songs,
Its healing vibrations.

Ride the drum
As you would ride a horse
On the infinite plains of life.

For the drum is your horse,
For the drum is your guide,
To spirit,
To yourself,
To the universe.

They are one and the same.

The drum is calling you home.

The drum is calling you home.

The drum is calling you home.

Can you hear it?

I surrender

To the grace
Of the universe

And all is well.

Thank you
For seeing me.

This is the most precious gift
One can ever receive.

I pray

For openness and softness of heart,

For sweet and deep human connections.

I pray

To embrace and honour long lasting commitments,

Ancient and ever-growing weavings.

I pray

To welcome the ephemeral,

The passing by,

The shooting stars,

The colourful butterflies,

The sweet scented breeze.

I pray

To learn

To let the go

And surrender.

I pray

To tap into

The uncanny essence of life,

The very nectar

That melts away

All forms of attachment.

I beg you dear heart,
Welcome me
And hold me
In your loving arms

When my body aches
And my mind goes
Round and round
Like a hamster wheel.

Hold me tight.

In the comfort
Of your love,
I surrender.

Wash my soul
With a rainbow.

Cleanse my thoughts
With a storm.

Caress my body
With sweet moonlight.

Heal my heart
With your song.

Sometimes
The only way forward
Is to find closure
For yourself.

To do
Whatever you need to do
To let go,
Bring peace
To your aching heart
And protective mind.

For this,
Call upon
Your spirit team.

Their help, guidance,
Support and love
Are always there for you.

Trust
Without an inch of doubt,

That together,

You can ride this wave

And reach a new horizon.

Prayers to the wind,
Thoughts from the bridge,

And rainbows as their magic echo.

Do not be sad,
I am with you.

And if you are to be sad,
Know that I am,
And will always,
Be with you.

I pray

To never

Feel the need

To try and explain

The magic

That is available to me,

That is given to me,

Each and every day.

Pray

With gratitude

And trust

Always.

For whether you are in pain

Or filled with joy,

The smile

You get from praying

With gratitude and trust

Radiates back

The universe's

Most golden nectar.

May my heart soften,

Expand and dance

With no trace

Of resentment

Or judgement

Left in it.

May I honour

Its right

To be loved,

Seen

And celebrated.

May I never forget

That it is deserving of this.

May I respect

Its wish for protection

And the wisdom

Of its own feelings, beatings and breathing.

May I trust

Its knowing,
My knowing.

May we grow
Together.

Grandfather Sun,

Let me bathe
In the warmth
Of your embrace,

Let me melt
In the soothing glow
Of your light,

Until I am ready.

Ready to go
Underground
Again.

May I trust
That there are
Collaborations
Out there
Hoping for me,
Waiting for me,

Just as I am
Hoping for them,
Waiting for them.

Aligned collaborations
In which it will
Feel safe
To be me,
In which I will dare
To take risks
And surrender
To the magic of creating
Something beautiful
With another being.
Something beyond our imagination.

Fragments Of Soul And Love Letters To Self

Feel the pain
Of not being seen
For who you are.

Breathe it out.

Come back home,
To the miracle
That you are.

You were never meant
To play small
My love.

You are after all,
Made of magic.

Sinking
Into my body.

Breathing
Into all the spaces,
All the cracks,
All the love
That keeps me alive.

Sinking
Into my body,
My spirit is free.

Hush now,
Sway gently,
Listen deeply.

You are all
That you should be.

Oh my love,
I love you so.

Let me wipe your tears
With the echo
Of your beauty.

Let me reach into your heart
With the resonance
Of your song.

You have no idea
How much we love you here.
You have no idea
How much you are valued here.

You have no idea
How essential you are
To the dance
Of the stars.

And so it is.

Hush now.
You are loved.

Sometimes things
Aren't done
Because of you,
But in spite of you.

Think about this
When you feel
Unworthy of love.

I find peace and comfort
In the unwavering beat
Of my own heart,

For it carries
Within itself
The heartbeats
Of all my ancestors,
Spirit guides,
The earth,
The stars,
And the entire universe.

There is no place
I'd rather call home
Than my own heart.

No clearer
Or stronger
Sense of belonging
Than that of being one
With the beat
Of the universe.

I was shown the door
To the secret garden of grace.

Never before had I imagined
How breathtaking and blissful
Pushing that door could be.

Never before had I imagined
How welcomed and celebrated
I would instantly be.

Never before had I realised
That grace
Was Alchemy.

As I caught a glimpse
Of the blossoms and scents,
All poison and resistance
Were transmuted,
And I was content.

Transported,

Transformed,
Reborn.

In a flip of a second,
I entered the garden

And grace took my hand.

You may not
Recognise me

But I am the one
Who whispered
Your name
In your dream

When you were lost
And didn't remember
You existed.

I cannot just be

The butterfly

That flies from

One flower

To another

And then leaves.

At some point

I need to become the bee.

I need to go back to the hive

And make honey.

I am

A channel

A crafter

A poet of life.

I believe
In change and spontaneity.

Yet, I am deeply grateful
For my ability
To persevere,
Work through,
And build.

Perhaps people
Are like streams.

Only a few are meant
To join your sacred river
And flow along
With you.

Sometimes

Admitting,
Respecting,
Honouring

The 'I no longer trust you' truth

Is the only way
The heart can feel
Safe enough
To heal.

One thing is for sure:

Unless we break through
The energy of stagnation

We cannot
Get any helpful
Answers.

When it comes to

Connecting

To our creativity

Or making positive

Changes

For oneself,

Most forms of resistance

Are but control

In disguise

Which itself

Is but fear

In a costume.

Have enough integrity
To love yourself deeply.

Anything
Less than this
Will lead to
Damaging behaviours,
Wounding of yourself,
And others.

I'm being called
To the mountains,
The sea, the rivers,
The fields and streams.

I'm being called to the Earth,
To lay in her arms and rest.

I'm being called
To the storms,
The winds, the rains,
The sunrays and snowflakes.

I'm being called to the Earth,
To lay in her arms and rest.

I'm being called
To the rainbows,
The stars, the moon,
The darkness and light.

I'm being called to the Earth,

To lay in her arms and rest.

To glance
At the sheer beauty
Of her infinite gift,
To feel
Her unconditional welcoming,
To know
Without an inch of doubt,

That She
Is also home.

Just like those wooden Russian dolls,

I inhabit this body,
Which inhabits the Earth,
Which inhabits the universe.

With a simple twist
Of perception,
I can clearly see

That the universe inhabits this Earth,
Which inhabits my body,
Which inhabits my spirit.

There is no linear way,
There is no separation.

All is one
Within the spiral
Of creation
And beauty.

Honour the wound

That lives

Beneath the need

To judge

And be right.

When we are
Calm and still enough
To receive the gift
Of a particular challenge,

We expand in places
We didn't even know existed.

I am bringing light
Into the cavern.

I will not
Let you down.

I sat and prayed
For the truth
To be revealed,
Whatever the truth may be.

My courage was rewarded
By the lifting
Of the weight
Of having to be right
And the fear
Of being wrong.

After that,
I was able
To stand
In a blissful state
Of trusting
That the universe knows,

And that truth
Will indeed
Be revealed.

Start each task
With a deep sense of gratitude,
And it will no longer be a task.

Embrace each difficult feeling
With a deep sense of gratitude,
And it will no longer be difficult.

Approach each dreaded conversation
With a deep sense of gratitude,
And it will no longer be dreaded.

Attend each impossible situation
With a deep sense of gratitude,
And it will no longer be impossible.

Difficult feelings
Aren't dangerous.

The real danger
Lies in the numbing,
The anaesthetising.

I hand over
With trust.

I let go
With grace.

I need to sit,

Quiet, raw, naked

And utterly devoted

To what is buried

And awaiting

To be reached,

Touched,

Revealed.

In reverence and gratitude

I welcome

The magic

About to unfold.

Our love

Grows

Tangible

In the space

Between

Worlds.

My dear little one

Who longs to play,
Who longs to be accepted,
Who longs to belong,

I hear you,
I see you,
I love you,

I bow to the beauty that you are.

I am here.

I will not leave.
I will not let you down.

My dear grown-up one

Who longs to play,
Who longs to be accepted,
Who longs to belong,

I hear you,
I see you,
I love you,

I bow to the beauty that you are.

I am here.

I will not leave.
I will not let you down.

Dear heart, soul, body, spirit,

I love you.

I enter the stillness you crave.
I step into the passion you long for.
I commit to the adventures you dream of.

I am here
With you,
For you.

I am your servant,
Your guide,
Your leader,
Your faithful cheerer.

I am cheering you on,
Right now.

I will not betray you.
I will not abandon you.

You are magnificent.

Your depth is a well
That feeds the ocean.

Your radiance a star
That makes other stars
Feel less lonely.

Your courage a force
That moves mountains.

You belong here.
You belong to all that is.

Love the self who feels.

It is time to accept,
Time to honour.

Accept all that you are.

Honour all that you have been given.

The stone you previously hid behind
Is now too small for this game,
The hole too narrow to go into.

You have grown dear one.
Grown far beyond what you can see,
Into the most magnificent rainbow.

Honour that.

Reclaim your beauty,
Your power,
Your brilliance,
Your true flame and fire.

You are a shooting star.
You are the Milky Way.

Do not play small.

This will neither serve you,

Nor God,

Nor others,

Nor the universe.

Remove

The obsolete programming

And strive.

Transmute

The old skins,

The old layers,

The old beliefs,

And rise.

I remember

The sweetness

Of being one with you,

Many lifetimes ago,

And I smile.

Today
More than ever,
I need to hug
My shadow.

The warmth

Of your embrace

Will always

Bring me

Back home.

I sit here
Drunk on a cocktail
Of fear and excitement,

Butterflies and knots
In my stomach,

Knowing that the big unknown
Is about to make its entrance.

I am a survivor
And a thriver.

The first does not
Compromise
The other.

But in the other,
Alchemizes
And courageously rises.

I hold

Myself

In my heart.

I once
Dreamt
Of being.

Now
I am.

I wove together
The wonders
All around me

And discovered,
To my biggest surprise,

That the very same tapestry
Lived
Inside of me.

Dear pain,

I hear you.
I hold space
For you.

I
Have
Reached
You
While
Finding
Myself.

In the depth

Of my aloneness

I never doubted

That you cared,

That you were near me

And that you truly loved me.

I find this quite extraordinary.

Feeling the pain
Does not prevent us
From being grateful
And positive.

It just helps us
Access
The vulnerability
Needed
To live
An authentic life.

Truth

May be

An illusion.

Nonetheless,

One must

Show up

And speak

One's truth

With deep courage,

Authenticity

And buckets

Of humility

Rather than

Judgement,

Arrogance

And condescendence.

Life

Is but a mystic dance.

I had turned

My dimmer down

So low

That I couldn't

See or remember

How or where

To switch on

The light.

I remember now.

Something beautiful happens in your life,

You are fully present,

You drink it in and smile,

Standing there

In pure radiance,

In deep acceptance.

Then you get worried,

You get frightened.

Perhaps the power of beauty scares you.

For beauty

Is the unknown

In all its glory,

And it can

And will change

Everything.

I might not be ready for this, what if...

The mind goes on alert,

It flashes protective signs, red lights
To build a barrier, a fence, a safe place.

But inside your heart,
There is more space than ever before,
More joy, more peace.

And your soul dances, sings and bounces
Like an excited dog,
So happy that his master has come home.

And your body softens, opens, realigns.

Let me tell you dear self,
There is space in you
For it all,

For the mixed feelings,
The confusion,
The certainty.

Allow them
To flow within you.

Feel what there is to feel
And let go
Of what no longer serves you,
Of what you know deep inside
Distorts everything else.

Do it
In your own time.

I believe in you.
I love you.

Let the anger be.

Let the pain be.

Feel them

As deeply

As you can

And rise

With the flames

Of bold energy

That are now

Burning

In ecstasy.

I sometimes long
To be the child
I left behind

When I was too young
To look after her.

I bow
To my body
For welcoming
My soul
So beautifully.

The comfort
Of your arms
Is like a night sky
Filled with stars.

Every now and then,
A shooting star
Goes right through my heart.

Wonder

Vagabond

Wanderer.

Such beautiful words.

Fire on.

My heart is
Bulletproof.

I think it is fair to say
That I have missed out
On being a princess
In this lifetime.

I'm fine with that.

Royalty doesn't do it for me anyway.

The Dance Of The Question

Is it rain

I hear

Falling

From your spirit?

An insight,

In this moment in time,

Can change history.

What is keeping you

From entering

The playground

Of a new creative adventure?

Be strict
With the thoughts
You welcome
Through your sacred door,

For they will take root
In your temple
And redecorate your heart.

Would you welcome them in your home
If they were in physical form?

If the answer is no,
Then you know what to do.

It is OK to be territorial about this.

It is OK to say no.

Once in,
The thoughts are very difficult to evict.

The protective ego
Has strong laws in place
To keep them striving
And you barely surviving.

So be strict
With the thoughts
You welcome
Through your sacred door.

There is always
A reason for things,
Always a bigger picture
Unfolding somewhere.

But it is not always
Our business
To know
What that reason is,

And we are not always
Ready
To embrace
The bigger picture.

Be patient with yourself.

Go beyond the personal

By diving

Even more deeply

Into the self.

Where does

The pressure

You feel put upon you,

Actually live?

Re-adjust

Your mindset

Before

It becomes

A minefield.

Which

Of your feelings

Are you

Listening to?

I dive deep
Into the energy
Of oneness,
Expansion
And bliss.

Live

With the questions.

Most answers

Are wrong.

I trust

That there was

Nothing

Left

There

To give

Or receive.

I do not understand
What is happening.

And that is
Completely
Fine.

First I thought
I was only
Heartbroken.

Now I know
I am also
'Heart-opened'.

Never was I more sure
Than when I was wrong.

How liberating
To laugh
At oneself,
To laugh
With oneself!

In the end

Isn't it just

About finding a way

That is

In alignment

And in tune

With our own unique being?

Live with the questions,
Do not fear them.

Their essence points you
In the right direction.

They are stepping stones
In disguise,

Leading you
To your sacred destination.

I looked out the window
To catch where the train
Was stopping.

But all I could see
Was an unidentifiable
Coffee shop.

Sometimes
The arrival point
Remains a mystery.

Clarity can either come
From having space,
Or from taking action.

Nothing in between.

What is love
But a magical door
Opening,

A sheer expansion
Of breath,

A full embrace
Of this very moment,

That happens again and again.

Life
Is sometimes
Messy.

That's OK.

You carry
The whole universe
Within you
My love.

What else
Do you need
To feel whole
And worthy?

Do you ever

Ask the stars,

Speak to them,

Listen to their message

And the echo

Of their dance?

Sometimes
It feels easier
To stay connected
To the light inside
While traveling.

Perhaps
Because of the gentle steadiness
And rhythm of movement.

Perhaps
Because of fresh, curious
And open eyes.

Perhaps
Because of an awakening
Of our sense of adventure,
Wonder and enthusiasm.

Perhaps
Because we become
As curious and open

As a child again,

With a joyful,
Excited heart,
And a renewed
Gift of observation.

What is the energy of excitement?

What is the energy of passion?

What is the energy of enthusiasm?

Are they one and the same?

Do they come from the same source
Or from different wells?

How can I fully honour it?

How can I fully honour them?

I watch the stillness of your body
As it lies here,
Deprived of breath.

It seems so strange to me
That your breath has left you,
That it has left us.

But has it really left?

And where did it go?

I can feel it merging
With my own,
Dissolving
Into oneness,
Filling the room.

You are even more here
In heart and spirit
Than ever before.

In this stillness
And emptiness,
Love
Is tangible.

And I wonder...

How does the breath
Transform so fast
Into another
Sacred element
As it leaves
Its earthly temple?

Perhaps it doesn't.

Perhaps it has always been
What it is to become?

Perhaps there has never been
Any separation
Apart from the one

In our human perception?

It seems impossible to me
That your breath
Would just vanish,

When it is the eternal
Carrier of Spirit.

And so it is.

Were we

On the same star?

Or were you

On the one

Right next to mine?

The questions themselves
Are sacred entities
And need no answers
To be complete.

Bow to them.

They may seem like
Unreachable mountaintops
But they are actually
Lighthouses
In the dark.

Trust and love them.

Within them
Is the key
To your treasure box.

Within them
Is the map
To where you need to go.

Live with the questions

Instead of trying so hard

To annihilate them

With very likely,

Distorted

Answers.

Can you taste

The fruit

When planting

The seed?

Have we met
Before,
A long, long
Time ago?

I seem to recall
The colour,
Flavour
And perfume
Of your dance.

What am I

But the reflection

Of your Divine love?

I choose
To keep diving
Deep
Into my own soul.

I am in awe
Of her intricate beauty.

A beauty
Fully interwoven
With yours,
And that of the souls
From infinite galaxies.

No question
Or answer
Is needed.

My soul has written

Millions of letters

To yours.

Does that mean

I am

Weird,

Mad,

Or perhaps

Both?

What is it
In your eyes
That tells me
We have met before,
Long ago,
In another life,
In another world?

Perhaps the answer
Lies in my own gaze.

Why is it

That we only

Believe

What we see,

What we are told

Or what has been

Proven to us

When the only place

Lies do not exist,

Is in the universe itself?

How far in

Does the sun go

When it penetrates

Our skin?

When it enters

Our heart?

Because it seems to me,

That there is

No limit

And yet

No exit.

Why is it

That I can see

Right into your soul

When I dive

Long and deep enough

Into your eyes?

I can hear
The whispers
Of the tree.

What is the sound
Of a tree laughing?

What is the sound
Of a tree crying?

What is the sound
Of a tree hugging?

What is the sound
Of a tree singing?

What is the sound
Of a tree healing?

What is the sound
Of a tree being?

What is the sound

Of the tree

Growing in me?

What is the sound

Of its whispers

Living in me?

What if each

Act of kindness

Does

Change the world?

Why are certain things

So hard to say

When they are

So easy to feel?

What if I were

A mere vagabond

On a bridge

With no other mission

Than to embrace

All that is.

Would you take my hand?

Because really,

This is what

And who I am.

Isn't it odd

That we often

Have more experiences

And adventures

In our dreams

Than in our awake state?

And yet,

There,

We rarely think

We need

To go and prepare ourselves

For years

Beforehand

In order to feel ready

To embrace

The unknown.

How does it

Really feel

To feel

Loved?

If you are you,
And I am I,

Then what
And who
Are we?

Why is it
That I have
Never
Believed in
Prince Charming,

And yet,
I believe
In fairy tales?

I was once

Innocence.

Since entering

Adulthood

Am I now

In 'non-sense'?

Why

Would there be

Less value

In a sentence

Written in the sand

Than one

Scribbled

On a piece of paper,

Or even

Embroidered in gold?

"I am the last survivor,"
My soul shouts.

"Of what?"
Says my heart.

What would I do

If I really loved

And valued myself?

This is the real question.

Don't

Most

Extra-ordinary

Things

Begin

With

The

Smallest

Ordinary

Step?

What and how

Am I to weave

So that the generations

To come

Are left with

Something worth

Not forgetting?

If we each come
To this Earth
With the essence
Of the whole universe
Within us,

Where have we
Foolishly
Discarded it
For some tasteless
Flavouring?

And how can we find it again?

When in deep silence,

Which one of us
Is talking?

Which one of us
Is listening?

What do you do

When the beauty

Of the butterfly

Has taken

Your breath away?

How will you

Hear me

If you keep

The noise up

So loud?

How will I

Hear you

If I keep

The noise up

So loud?

I like to think

That the struggles

Linked to

Being an idealist

Are more

Worthwhile

Than the ones

That come from

Being too much

Of a perfectionist.

And yet who knows...

I might be completely deluded!

Where

Do goodbye songs

Go?

How can I taste

The honey

From the nectar

Of my joyful heart?

How does

One know

Not to add

That extra brushstroke

To the perfect painting?

Epilogue

My hope is that after reading theses pages you may remember the wonders of your whole being, the power of your own medicine and feel able to tap into the well of your unlimited healing, mystery and potential.

May you feel empowered to explore, trust and fully live this beautiful life you have been given.

You are the miracle.

You are the medicine.

I look forward to our meeting with book 3 when I will, no doubt, see you fully showing up and shining your light in the world.

You are the enchanted forest that the world needs.

Dedication

I would like to dedicate this book to all the beautiful souls on both sides of the veil, who inspire me to look for my own healing balm, who give me some of theirs when I find it difficult to access mine, who consistently remind me that help is available and that I can choose hope and trust over victimhood and scepticism.

With all my heart, Thank you.

A massive thank you to my dear partner, friends and family who stand by me, believe in me and let me do my thing no matter what (whether they have a choice in this last matter is another question! I am rather stubborn!). I would also like to thank all the people I have met on the way who have really seen me and have cheered me on, whether in person or on-line. You all matter. Huge gratitude to every single person who has contributed to my funding campaign to self-publish this set of three books. Lastly I'd like to give a massive heartfelt shout-out to the fabulous Tanya Markul for getting me and my creations and helping me produce and bring together this series of three books in a way that I am super excited about and proud of.

And to you who is reading this, I honour and celebrate the beautiful and unique person that you are. May you always be reminded that you matter and are worthy of all of life's magic and healing balm.

About The Author

Natacha Dauphin is a singer-songwriter, sound channel who believes her craft is a bridge between worlds, that the words in her books were sent as letters from her ancestors, the life around her, and spirit. Events and circumstances meant she had to grow up too quickly, but always felt guided inwardly—to strive for peace and forgiveness versus resentment and bitterness, which has allowed her to explore the artistry of her wounded journeys with comfort, spaciousness, and possibility. She feels emotional wounds are beautiful and mysterious, and hold precious keys to leading a freer, more authentic, joyful life. She also believes in miracles, creativity, and the power of the human heart. She's now living her own dream by sharing her books, helping others find their voice, and embracing every minute of her time here on Earth.

www.natachadauphin.com

Have you read 'Letters From The Wound', volume 1
of *The Soul Letters You Never Received* series?

***

Find it on Amazon

Or

contact me directly to get your copy at:

honouringyourcreativefire@gmail.com

www.natachadauphin.com

Printed in Great Britain
by Amazon

82630406R00133